Verity is Relative: Emma's Memoir

by

e. smith sleigh

Poetry Books:
THESE THINGS are a One Thing©
OUR NATURE: External Landscapes©
THIS NATURE: Internal Landscapes ©
MUSINGS FROM
THE FAULT LINE AFTER DARK©
AN AMERICAN STILL LIFE©

For images, excerpts, a blog, illustrations
and ordering information visit
the website
http://esmithsleigh.weebly.com/

Artistrie & Associates

2018
Revised

To **Truth**, if it exists
To **Love**, however temporary

To mother Earth
and Father Time

Truth is verity
verity is sometimes long-lived
but more often not

I've been called a survivor, guess I am. I'm an author, a poet and a non-fiction writer. I write twenty-first century poetry. I'm a post-structuralist proponent and an arts advocate.

I spent the first half of my adult life learning and traveling. And, I spent the second half of my life writing about those experiences.

Below is a life story--some bits and pieces of an existence that was quite an endeavor. I hope that in the telling of it, some will be inspired to travel, to cope with loss, to hate appropriately, to love passionately, or embrace Post-structuralism as a style.

The poetry in this book is presented in columns. the prose runs from margin to margin. You are looking at a future book with meanings that are the reader's task to decipher. A post-structural theorist might talk about the playfulness of language, style, structure, and the structure of language and the book.

My Best,

Emma

Part I
Home Life

Maryland

standing in the middle of this little lane rather than the sound of a breath taken rather than the beat of my heart I feel the hush

I feel the grey autumn evening wrap around me the way a cool evening envelops you in its heaviness lets you know you are not where you're supposed to be

the sun begins to set primal instincts take over in your head and send you home

during your run home from your friend's house you stop to look at the waves and hear the water lap the shoreline

when you finally notice dim evening close 'round you you leave land's edge and take off for home

when you're running that fast you pretend you can fly you always pretended that you could fly in your waking hours in your dreams you run you take off you soar

you try to beat the sunset home because you don't want to displease your mother by returning to your house after dark

home is a white clapboard-sided house with a field stone foundation outside inside is a fieldstone fireplace your house is located by the Chesapeake Bay mom's in the kitchen with a beautiful smile on her face she's wearing her white frilly apron which means we have company or she made an extra good meal for us tonight

but you suspect something you're uneasy it's that unsettled feeling you'll recognize for the rest of your days

little brother's in the living room playing with the small plastic soldiers that he loves he's not supposed to play in there he's singing first verses of all the military fight songs

Dad has a long commute he's not home from work ...

that's not really the way it was   except for the field stone   the plastic
army men   your dad's commute   oh yea and   the flying
thing that's true and your mother well, you haven't a clue about
her except   day by day since your birth she drew you deeper and
deeper into the absurdities that made up her thoughts

when something happened good   or bad   she verbally molded and
defined the event to fit the moment or the occasion   and you were
advised "this must be told this way   you have to tell it exactly like this
we keep things to ourselves   no one knows our business but us
everything is fine   remember that   we're just fine"

your Dad never made it home that night

your father was all that stood between you and your mother
and he was gone

your gut says your mother discerned he'd never come home   she
always celebrated that night

you never found out why

passage

and where are we today

take this tome from my hand
we will visit earth
and walk through the human world

hear the verse   feel the beauty
consider   understand revere
fear

breathe baby

brick wall makes you hyperventilate
closed in   close   too close

glass blocks look like an opaque
non-world
like the world of an infant fighting to see
fighting to hear
confused at the
confusing

red brick
the color of the womb

translucent

yes   you remember
you heard
you wonder

vistas

on this mesa   at the brink of this expanse   this great loneliness
a large stone jutting upward near the ledge's end   you're teetering
there's loose gravel underfoot   you keep your balance by placing your
hand on the large rock

finally seated on the mesa's outcropping   you're reminded that in the
Southwest   you always feel imminent death   all things fight for
existence here   through long stretches of time   barren distances
and lack of water for hundreds of miles

like most humans clinging to *Tierra Madre* for life, the infant clutches
its mother who holds the child close to protect it from the sand in the
wind

you cling to the large rock beside you   and look down   even life in a
desert is indisputable and abundant in its own way   yet expendable in
an instant

before you   the dry winds blow stronger across the scorched expanse
but you cannot make yourself leave this spot where the hypnotic
colors of the sunset celebrate   existence   red   orange yellow
lavender   and pink dance over the landscape   into the grey horizon
you bath in beauty and the evening breeze

you send your adoration of mother earth outward   across land   and
time   into the dry infinite   you cling to the boulder feet dangling
toward solid ground   hundreds of meters below   you watch a dust
devil   you feel the swirling wind play life   play death   dance with
spirits

more rocks on the cliff's edge shift and crash into the darkening depths
below

but there is no *conclusión*

not today

child's play   not largesse

on your journey down the path   you pretend you're swinging a stick at
an egg in an ancient-looking nest

you want to live with song, light beams, contentment   song
but you break the egg's shell   anyway

a full-size dragon inside the egg awoke   its breath blasted fire at you
it told you to put the stick down and shut up   for some reason you did

you started a deadly high stakes chess game with the dragon   you
looked down

you should have looked up   you should have looked around for an
answer   to ascertain the why   the how to leave

at first nothing happened   but the dragon followed you home and
rebuilt its nest in your backyard   in your brain   it ate chicken soup on
occasion

your song was invalidated   degraded   you were sent to the Alice-moon
the dragon attempted damage of some kind to you all the time all
along the way   your journey was constantly disrupted and judged

you longed for the dragon to die   burned by its own fire   you wanted it
to leave   it didn't   until almost the end

that dragon was the main reason your life played out the way it did
your archeology became a stew pot   a vessel bereft of an anchor   a
fight for survival   an out of tune hum a non-song

mislaid plans   a mission gone wrong

July

mirages of water on hot asphalt
hot seats in the car
steam bath days
dewy dark nights
gardens prepare to ripen
a holiday for the country
male family members' birthdays

full green foliage on the trees
sun hats baseball caps
shorts

you soar in a swing
fly on a bicycle
you plunge off a diving board

keeping the bird bath full
bay breezes that push hot mid-days away
the smell of suntan lotion

cold air conditioning   after going inside
thirst for lemonade   or sweet tea
spitting watermelon seeds

bare watermelon rind
upturned in a smile on the plate
lists of light meals   cucumber salads
smell of tomato plants on your hands

all received in a prescription for July

the chicken

on a cloudy day in late spring at your great aunt and uncle's house
a turn of the 20th century craftsman structure your mother led you
and your brother outside into the white picket-fenced backyard

a vegetable garden grew in the back flower beds were planted along
the fence and in the yard's center your grandmother's red rose bush
grew it was your favorite

you stared at the large red blossoms eventually you walked over to
touch one of the buds and smelled it you were lost in delight

unnoticed by you or your brother your mother walked into the white
clapboard garage that sat off the alley behind the house when she
came out she carried a wooden crate inside was a chicken you
couldn't believe it a real live chicken to pet

you ran over to your little brother to ask him if he thought Mother
would let you touch it or play with it

your mother interrupted "I'm going to teach you how to kill a chicken"
quick as a ninja she opened the door and reached into the cage she
caught the chicken by the neck in a nano second the chicken was
squawking at the top of her voice

you and your little brother started screaming your mother twirled the
chicken in the air by its neck around and around after what seemed
a long time the poor chicken died killed by our mother's hands

"why" you scream "why"

"we're going to eat that bird today"

you both scream again "no no noooo"

she left you and your brother out in the yard
you were left with the searing pain of her slap on your face

she stomped away she was at all times disappointed in you
she always let your brother and you know that it was all your fault
when something went wrong

in other cultures killing a chicken in front of children may be a frequent occurrence but for you   it wasn't

the situation seemed brutal to you   one more reason to be afraid that some similar event could happen to you

comments by my mother after hearing the above read to her: "you've always been obsessed by that goddamned chicken   it's dead   it's dead yes   I killed it and some of us ate it"

rebuttal: there was a grocery store a few blocks away   she had the money to purchase a chicken and an automobile to drive there

speed bumps

wasn't long after you could hold a dialogue with your little girl self
that you figured out there was something off about your mother

she was so calmly unkind when no one was present or listening
reptile-like she would wait in ambush for just the right moment to
strike

you were her chief prey her prey of choice but there were many
others on her menu mostly relatives sometimes you felt sorry for
them

you felt strangely detached from the predatory attacks from her mouth
mostly her mouth sometimes her hands the switch a belt the
incidents were yours and her relatives to hide

even now when you write about her you feel you must hide what
she perpetrated you never let yourself feel sorry for her she desired
that above all things to be the victim in every situation
that was her goal her cover her feigned state of suffering

she was so good at pretending to be the injured party
you supposed something imaginary was so much easier for
visitors to believe than the truth you couldn't believe no one
guessed the truth

you never trusted the deluded do-gooders she invited to the door
the Medieval town's people come to visit the kind dragon you always
wondered why they never noticed the bruises or the lies in the room

you built a wall to shield yourself from the lack of truth in your life
from her the wall took a great deal of effort to construct but you
did build it that stone fortress remains around you to this day

e raced the word

scorched   scored checked   flags flying
in your dreams somebody wins

some moments in life take a run at you
like a race car

you stand in the middle of the track
your feet are stuck in the pavement

you can't move   the flag dropped
there it is   automobiles race toward you
at an astounding   immeasurable velocity

of course you only have one option
pull your feet out of the muddy slowmo sludge

and fly

just remember not to hit the wall
you won't survive

will you even try

the price of the moon

things are so bad around here
that you have to raise your arm
with the injured shoulder and
push up to support the moon

unstable air inside and outside
the house   the usual torment
destabilized your birthday
threats of tornados outside
rain in torrents

torrent of emotions inside
insanity emotions from dictated life
undecided content to drink: mix two parts
toxic paranoia into one part psychosis

Tony Bennet washes over you
'I found you just in time, you made
my lonely life that lucky day' uh huh
now that you think about it   dipping
heel   your toes   then feet into the waters
of endurance was a good idea

you yell "call me Not-Achilles"

within an e-mail two years ago:

"I'm happy to answer your request, darling.
My response is below. Hugs and Kisses ..."

Central Park

I've known her for a long time   we met in college

it seems to me   if I recall correctly she was always throwing
something   she played championship softball and intramural
volleyball and possessed a wicked tennis game

at a NYC party she tossed a boomerang kiss across the room at me
it hit the mirror and sailed back to her

she poured a bucketful of water down her dorm's ninth floor waste
chute and listened as it gained speed in its hurtle toward the bottom
and a caught-gawking janitor

she threw huge pine cones instead of panties out a fifth floor window
during an attempted panty raid

she sat silent while Wade told her   his sexual preference wasn't...
her...   she threw every shoe in her closet at him

she fell asleep in the Louvre's dining area because her thoughts
about the *Winged Nike of Samothrace* engulfed her
in pleasure   she felt at ease there   in that building   finally
something so familiar   so real   something that was hers

it wasn't

she cried for three weeks when the department chair told her to
choose her children or a PhD   she said no to him several times   he
knew what he was doing   if she chose her children Emma would
lose her career a discipline that she loved and pursued since she was
twelve years old

she threw a fit   as they say   but who could blame her   she chose her
children

when her three year old said daddy touched me there   she told the bastard she was going to move out of the house with the children and he wasn't going to stop them   the toooo important perv-asshole climbed to number one on her list

she bought a voodoo doll and aimed negative thoughts that flew like pins into him   he never visited the children   he finally died of an utterly foul gangrene called wretchedness

she lobbed a rock into the grand canyon   and listened to it rumble   out of sight   she vowed she would never return   she said something about the abyss's edge representing failure

in a nearby town's gift store she selected a lined tablet and an exquisite pen that streamed velvet ink from the tip   with it she began to write like she never wrote before

she called a 'jet-setting' Swiss publisher by another name then fucked him all over a suite in the Tunis Hilton

she told me these stories and more in the Park   she kissed me with the softest   lushest lips   then turned toward the museum

she air kissed the right person that night from across the room   my timing was off   the mirror cracked when I turned for one more …
chance
glance
catch of a reflected kiss

she's a hero   I know   she knows   how to survive   how to throw

kisses like boomerangs

-- your friend,
Ash

Datura

she grew there between the hard stones
it was Purple Datura   poisonous   but pretty
she trades on the pretty

purple siren   she will beckon you to touch her
you know   she loves acquisition
the house   the things   the bud kids
the rings   lots of rings

as a rule Datura becomes bored with it all
she finds no significance in attained ownership
possession to her is the act   the act of...
the Act

weary from her recreation
Purple Poison returns to her natural state
those who touched her
walked on her   tasted her
plucked her from her wall of stone
always fall   she suffers no regrets

no compunction comes
with the poison   the gift

rejoice

this is her chosen life cycle

"we keep things to ourselves
no one needs to know about this
everything is fine   we're fine
remember that"

desert

you lived
in
a desert of intelligence
and
like the lost
in a sand desert
you were just as thirsty

in that desiccated land
parched lips
of despair
cannot be slaked

zigzag

suncast shadows drawn by the blinds on the window frame flashed the pointed teeth of a pumpkin carved by you and your husband-to-be the maple leaves fell intertwining you played at being children one last time nothing warned you about the ending to the story

suncast shadows drawn by the blinds on the window frame flashed the rose color mountain peaks your house faced in Arizona some cultures' proverbs instruct 'never oppose a mountain' you wish you knew that when you lived there

suncast shadows drawn by the blinds on the window frame flashed the stacked floors of an ultra modern twentieth century grey-blue steel and glass high-rise you inhabited in Europe for a short time an experiment in living it swayed when the winds blew

suncast shadows drawn by the blinds on the window frame remind you of sharks teeth on the sidewalk crafted with chalk by the neighbors' children

suncast shadows drawn by the blinds on the window frame remind you of rickrack applied to your grandmother's apron

suncast shadows remind you of the desert mountain lion chasing a rabbit around parked cars their zigzags remind you of a border design on a late eighties memo pad
tire treads shoe soles
stair risers to nowhere
or Quetzalcoatl ascending to a
Mayan heaven or descending to its equivalent hell

suncast shadows drawn by the blinds on the window frame remind you of multiple performance stages

suncast shadows create zigzagged, indistinct platforms of memory

When I weathered the **storms** in my young life and made it through high school, I was surprised.

My mother still tried to meddle in my life. During my public school career, she gave me little help with my school work or activities, so I hung out at the library.

She was helpful to me, only at times, when her actions somehow benefited her. During my freshman and sophomore years in high school, she encouraged me in an off-hand way.

"Keep going. You can make it 'til you're sixteen, then you can leave, that's the law." My mother loathed reading, rejected learning, she only like the socialization. I loved academics. I defied her.

With the help of a few of her relatives, especially my mother's older brothers, and a boy named Wade, whom I met on a hayride when we were both high school sophomores, I graduated and went on to college.

Wade and my relationship became complicated when two weeks before the start of our freshman year in college, he confided in me that he might change his sexual orientation.

good-bye

the windows melted like cheese in tuna melts they were opaque
like eggs cooked on a hot august sidewalk melted dark like chocolate
left in the backseat of a car liquefied margarine in the grocery bag in
summer like ice cream melted, sticky on the sidewalk

I melted me suspended me dissolved my instinct said run but
my mind told me to stay no definition for this sad so sad sadness
could be found within the dictionary of hurt

what will happen I asked is this really happening...this...what is this...

leave stay leave stay leave
stay melt fly
fly go
go
away

for Wade
a slip back in time

we race across the field on horses   wind blowing through long hair
no saddles   no dressage

we brace ourselves with taut thighs and our knees we jump the
hedges in a wild charge   us   abandoned to speed   we take flight
in a moment of danger   and exultation

I glimpse   a forgotten rock quarry we run   plunge over the old
limestone cliff into the clear azure water below   rush of wind
in our ears   everlasting emotion

I feel a long kiss   empty lake house high front deck we hang over it
a cool wind blows along the water's edge   just as our lips meet

on a cold night we walk across town wrapped in layers of clothing
overheated we jump into a snow bank   snow falls into our mouths
while we sing   let it snow   let it   snow   let   it   snooow

on this summer day I want to touch the sweat in your belly button
brush away wet hair from your face   I want to feel the heat of your
body again

I want to breathe the winter's cold   I miss the intensity of your
warmth   you are the best of summer heat and the deadliest of
wintry frost
to me   here
and you're not

in this hot summer's day

modifications

change what
my home for a parachute

saying goodbye to the shiny things
yes I'm traveling straight on
changing nests changing dwellings
like clothes I'm changing
I'm changing spaces

up all night reading maps
plotting the life

refueling in mid-air exiting faster
and faster returning through wormholes

springing into quantum effects
levitation of the Casimir kind

settling settling
but not down
hovering
covering what used to be known
as ground

Part II
College Life

No one possesses the power to change your situation except you

abduction

I hear something like a body
falling through branches
on its way to the woodland floor
I feel the plummet of my heart
it hits the well of my stomach

I feel that sinking feeling it's a warning
when a dangerous love approaches
an odd love   a new love
a risky love   a love I need
a love almost impossible to reject

a zombie apocalypse love
that could cost me everything
or help me gain the whole thing
oh   reason once bearing my mind aloft

you flew out the door

you flew away

When I entered the university where Dr. Seebeck taught, I was barely 18 and he was 37. I was drawn to him immediately. I fell in love with his voice.

I heard his voice delivering knowledge to me in the darkened room of my art history class (yes, art history). The timbre of it rose and fell, beguiled me, and lingered in my mind. I felt all the subtle nuances of his speech. I relished everything he said.

I found the sumptuous images in front of me on the screen so beguiling. The wonderful, sexy voice behind me, presenting the knowledge that I sought, seduced me. I took in the information like a sponge. His words poured into my mind. He transported me to places and revealed things to me I never experienced before.

I studied his looks and his manner. I admired the way he commanded attention when he walked into a room. Did I mention I liked his voice? He was highly intelligent. He had the answers to so many things. He excelled in the field I longed to enter.

The day he handed-out the first graded tests of the semester, I summoned the courage to speak to him. As soon as I looked through the test, I realized I didn't know how to answer his exam questions.

I went up to him after class. I told him that the test format was new to me. I simply didn't know how to take his tests. I apologized for my low grade. I told him I felt as though I learned more than was evidenced by my grade. When I ended my short monologue, I said something like, "Please tell me what you want."

He smiled at the floor and then laughed a little nervous laugh.

"All right," he replied. “I’m going over to the library. Would you like to walk with me?”

I was not aware of the *double entendre* I spoke. I was still *naive* about a great deal of life. He wasn’t. He was my instructor in so many things and my instruction began that day.

Connecticut

He invited me to walk over to the library with him. The afternoon was late and the sun was setting. The fall leaves crunched beneath our feet. They fell in a golden shower as we walked. His stride was so proud. I matched his pace.

In the library, he showed me the resources I needed to know about his, my, discipline: the use of a library for studying, researching, and writing. He told me about the different approaches to art historical research.

He took me to the stacks and we walked through them. As we walked, he gave me so much information. He told me how to take tests, and not just his tests. I would have spent months trying to glean this information from of my classes.

He sensed I reveled in the wonderful compelling field called art history. We didn't have to speak about it. We walked together and eventually sat down to look at a few large books.

The sexual tension between us built all that evening. I needed to touch him and feel my response as he touched me.

When he wasn't looking, I would close my eyes for a moment as I did in his classroom and feel his lush, deep voice penetrate my being.

I brushed his hand with mine as I reached for a book, it was electric. I sat there with a need for him like nothing else, for no one else, ever, in my life. My desire grew even stronger when I tried to hide the feeling from him. I felt as if I were ready to burst. I wanted to burst.

I know he felt the tension, too. As he talked to me, he studied my face and looked deep into my eyes. He studied me even more when I looked away. These were the moments that changed my life.

The Seal

Eventually, he stood.

"I have a book in my office that I want to give you. It's entitled How to Beat Test Anxiety. Would you like to go back with me now to the fine arts building or, well, we could, perhaps, I could give it to you after the next class."

I paused before I answered. I was almost sure I knew what he was saying. I had to do a little check with myself. Do you, can you, will you, won't you? Nothing mattered. I wanted him.

"Your office is on my way back to the dorm, I can go with you now."

I watched him slip his key into the lock of the classroom door. It was so sexy. Everything was sexy to me during those moments I was first alone with him.

His office was behind a very large, theater of a classroom. He didn't turn on the lights, but took my hand and led me through the darkness to a dim light in the hallway above his office door. I watched him slide another key into his office lock. He pushed the door open then turned to me. He took my hand again.

I thought he was going to lead me into his office. Instead, he led me several feet down the hallway to the right side and into the darkness. He grabbed both my wrists and pinned my hands above my head on the wall.

His whispered in my ear, "Who are you and what are you doing to me?"

I laughed very quietly. With my voice just as sexy and low as his, I whispered, "You know perfectly well who I am. I'm the one who's going to fuck you tonight and all the rest of your days."

He whispered, "Call me Luke when we're together." He smelled my hair.

"I have to touch you now. I've wanted to touch you since I first saw you. Don't say anything else, just let it happen."

His one hand held my wrists against the wall above my head. The other hand moved to my face, his two fingers traced the curves of my cheek to my lips.

One of his fingers circled my lips. They moved to my ears and my neck. His hand moved down to my blouse. The top of his hand brushed against my nipples' arousal. He felt under my arms, over each breast, and down my sides.

With his full palm, he pressed down my stomach to my navel and down to the edge of my skirt. He raised my skirt and his hand went to my panties. I know he felt my wetness. He slid his hand between my legs.

He rubbed my thighs and legs with his fingertips as far as he could reach then traced and retraced the lines he drew on my body. His hand moved up my other side. He continued his exploration. I was full of need for him.

I sensed he wanted me to resist a little, so I did. My resistance made him more vigorous in his movements. He pressed his entire body up against me to hold me still. He tightened his grip on my wrists. His strength and hardness sent shivers through my body to my toes.

He became a little rougher. He kissed my lips with a kiss that could melt steel. He sucked on my lower lip. His tongue penetrated my mouth.

He moved his mouth to my breasts and lightly bit the hardened tips of my nipples through my clothing. My clit was pulsating. He started undressing me. He tore at my clothing. Before I knew it, I was standing nude in the hall.

"I want you." He took his pants off.

I looked at his erection and wondered if I could take all of him. When he lifted me off the ground and slammed me against the wall. He kissed my body all over. He prepared me for what was next.

He carried me into his office and sat in an armless chair he used for reading. He lifted me onto his erection, inch by inch. I took it. Ahhh, the exquisite pain. I slid down on him. He played with my clit rubbing it up and down with one short vibrating stroke after another. He continued with a light steady rhythm behind it.

My entire body started to quake, I moved on him like an inhuman force. I wanted what was about to happen. My clit was hard. The pressure built and built then came the merciful, exquisite release.

He placed his hand over my mouth and whispered with that divine voice, "You cannot scream."

I did anyway. He muffled my sounds and pumped even harder. His hands fell away from my mouth. We groaned together in rhythm with our sex. His climax was shattering for both of us.

We held each other. My body pressed against his. I had never felt complete oneness with another human being, not like that. He knew exactly what I liked without my having to tell him.

We stayed in the chair, wrapped around each other for a while. Then, I stood. He studied me like the images he displayed on the huge classroom wall. I let him. I reveled in his gaze. I watched him grow hard again.

A feeling inside overwhelmed me. You know the one. I wanted more. He knew it. He stood up and put his hands on my shoulders. He spun me around; and, with his hands on my hips at my pelvis, he pulled me to him. He pressed himself against me, and walked me to his desk.

He nuzzled my ear with his face in my hair and whispered, "Lean over this. I'm going to take you from behind."

He pushed against my back with his hand and bent me over. I was ready and wanted to feel him pushing into me. I wanted to feel him pulsing with heat.

From behind, he felt even larger. Sensations overwhelmed me. This time my own hand covered my mouth. We climaxed together. He started kissing my back all the way to my ass. He stood up, turned me around, and pulled me to him.

"I don't want to stop."

He whispered, "there are a few things we'll save for another time."

He held me while we came down from the most incredible sex of our lives. How do I know? He told me. I believed him. He talked to me so softly. His voice surrounded me in a deep, rich melody of words. I felt nothing but bliss.

I adored our sex together. Every encounter we had was always good, no matter what age or where we were. It was good.

He taught me that sex is an art form. It was performance. Any consentient sex performed well was an affirmation of life. He instructed me in the art of ultimate pleasure for both sexes. He taught me an almost infinite variety of skills. His knowledge and imagination held few boundaries. Luke trained me to see and feel the sensuality of life.

He fueled my desire, my libido. My pleasure was knowing I could give such pleasure. My confidence in my sexuality enriched our lives.

good

the poetic ancients along the Nile declared to their lovers
"you are the ben ben of my soul"
do you not love their dance   their writing on stone walls

on waves   words float from continents
over land   in the waves of grasses

heat   or warm waters   heated bodies
beneficial heat   good   glorious sex in our pool of soothing waters
benevolent   benign reassuring

study entomology   Middle English _boon_ ("prayer") from Old Norse
bón ("prayer, petition")   from Proto-Germanic *_bōniz_ ("supplication")
*_bʰā_- ("to say") influenced by _boon_ ("good, favorable", adj.)

Cognate with Swedish _bön_ ("prayer, petition, request")
Danish _bøn_ ("prayer")
Old English _bēn_ ("prayer, request, favor, service")   benefit

he _is_ the _ben ben_ of my soul

Sussurrus

my soul is pierced by your eyes
they slide into my mind
my longing for you burnishes my core
you've awakened my spirit
you fulfill my every yearning and need
I am wrapped in the mystery of you

when my passion increases
you counter
sensuous   irresistible

the price I pay for the delight of you
is damnation   I care not
for you are my inexplicable bliss
eternity is caught in our sighs

this hidden place is veiled
in whispers of our love
we belong here   swathed in tranquility
captured by our susurrant *concord*
within this seduction   this secrecy

I run to your body
to quit the burdens of life
to lie in dewy clouds
to become cloaked in dewy mists
you are my completion and desire
my life is renewed   by your love

appearance

While searching through papers in their office at Emma and Luke's vacation home, Mitch, Luke's son, found photos of Emma mixed in with the post cards she sent Luke. Whatever the hair length or color, or the type of dress, or the continent she walked upon, she always looked good. Luke once said she sparkled. In some of the photos, she was stunning.

Emma was never rail-thin like some of the women Mitch's age tried to become. She looked good, healthy. She had a good attitude about herself and she came off very confident and sexy. She had a great sense of humor, too. It showed. Her smile was mischievous.

parameter dissonance

she's seeking new sensations
just when there are fewer smoky rooms
jazz   rock and roll   sleek fast cars
boxes of t-bones   caviar and eggs
chateaubriand for two   silver trayed *bonbons*

recherché la Liberté
creativity regulated interrupts the flow

most things regulated are a no go

don't tell her now that life and time will hurt
what will she do when she can't play
when her arms are aching
what does she reach for

tell her to ignore the pain and
go for the amusement
allow her to find her time uncomplicated

uninterrupted

Mitch is Luke's Child

In many ways, Emma was an enigma to Mitch. She had always been in his life. Luke first told him about her when he was very young. She was Luke's favorite student and considered a family friend.

Mitch never really understood the relationship between the two of them. He knew Luke wanted to help her. Mitch thought it was a student/professor thing. After she graduated from college and went on to graduate school, Luke and Emma continued to stay in touch.

No matter where she was or what she was doing, Luke was interested in what was going on with Emma. He was involved in her life.

Luke taught in one college all his life, lived in one town, with one house, one wife--until she died, and one son. Luke was an academic and, at that time, he was subject to the unyielding demands and regulations concerning relationship with students.

Emma explored her world, the worldly world. Luke encouraged her. Her adventures were important to both of them. She had adventures when traveling was easy and more secure. Flying was an experience, something you dressed for and enjoyed. Threats from different parts of the world were fewer. The foremost international problem for the United States was the old Soviet Union.

reverie

they were the halcyon days
somehow there and yet to come

they were joyful days full of contentment
the beauty of fine art relished
life tasted   uninhibited freedom of movement
affection and love for one another

the halcyon days were
somehow there and yet to come

the weather was deep blue skies
and rolling thunderstorms
the air pleasant to swim through
breathe in
the sunlight was a lush gold
green colors sparkled   evoked happiness
we could roll on grass lawns
down the grassy hills

those were days of careless wonder
                    of careless wandering
they were the halcyon days
days that were here
and there
and somehow yet to come

we lived by the light of millions of stars
millions of radiant suns that gilded our nights
                                gilded our lives

they were somehow there   yet to draw near
and still to come

their days were driven by the pulse of a different,
a distant thrum

Son

Before he retrned to the city, Mitch walked into the office and library. He entered the room and paused at the desk.

Emma and Luke displayed their family and travel photos on the desktop and in the bookshelves. Family images were scattered among their certificates and degrees. Photos also hung on the walls.

Emma mounted the documents and pictures in frames. They ranged in style from antique to contemporary. They told a story, the history of a family.

A childhood picture of Mitch hung there. He saw another picture, his favorite photo of his dad, himself, and his kids. He took the photo off the hanger and studied it. He shook his head from side to side.

He sighed. "*Life...*"

Mitch looked at photographs of Luke and Emma in various locations. A photo of Emma when she was young rested on the desk along with another one of Emma's children when they were toddlers. A beautiful frame held one of Isabel's pictures when she was about three.

Kathryn's portrait at sixteen years stood there in a similar frame. A photo of Emma holding a baby held a prominent position on the shelves just behind the desk. It stood out from the rest. In the photo, Emma looked wistful, almost sad.

Part III
a family to love

newness

a foggy dawn
emerged
out of the night

it is
cool and quiet
peaceful and green

in this midsummer
the fog erases
all the blemishes
and leaves the newness
of a newborn baby

with all the possibilities

ever

some say love lasts forever
but forever is relative

I've known minutes
that were forever

I can still
feel them

where is he
I keep questioning

Like any male, **Mitch** read passages of books or magazine articles just because they were sexy, but he did not know the people who wrote them. What he read in the files stacked on his father's desk were personal accounts of their intimate lives from family members. He reasoned his father wanted him to read the files, to understand...something.

These are such private papers. I never really paid much attention to things like this. Perhaps Dad wanted me to understand how intense his relationship with Emma was, from their first encounter. But, why?

After going through some of the papers in the file, Mitch came across a handwritten, then photocopied journal entry his father wrote:

"I offer no excuses for loving Emma. I offered no excuses for loving someone much younger than I am. This young woman completes me. She fascinates me. I hear her laughter and I myself am young. She offers me comfort and intelligence, acceptance and responsiveness. She is non-judgmental. Her needs and desires are my needs and desires.

I require nothing but to be near her."

Further into the journal entries, Mitch found this:

"Emma was everything I wanted in a partner. She was inquisitive, and interested in what I said. She possessed an intuitive response to anything visual.

Her pursuits were our pursuits. Her natural sexiness drew men to her. While she was in college, I watched her charm so many of her classmates. She showed very little sexual interest in them.

I knew she was mine. From the first moment we met, we wanted each another every day of our existence. The first few years of our relationship were intense.

When we were together, she was like a drug to me. She was highly addictive. I wanted no one but her. Her responses to me were incredible. I lived for our moments alone. I dreamed of a time when, at last, we could be together permanently.

I should have faced down the forces that tried to impose their skewed morality on us. I should have divorced Angela and made Emma my wife early on.

When we were older, I tried to make up for what we lost. Other than our children, she is my life."

He went on to describe their meetings all over the United States. Mitch was amazed at the times and places they were together. He never had a clue when he was growing up that they were in love.

After reading just a few of the pages in his journal, he understood. My father's thoughts were with her. His preoccupation was Emma. Guess that's why I was jealous of her at times.

Mitch also discovered this **note**:

Dear Emma,

Your birthday is tomorrow. I wish you the best.
I've sent a birthday card to you and a small gift.
I hope you can wear it at times to remind you
of our love.

He briefly shuffled through the papers. There's a lot of correspondence between them here. I should have guessed some of this stuff. Several of their meetings occurred during his international trips. They met all over the world.

Even though Dad was much older than Emma, it's obvious they were sexually compatible. Sex was like a chess game for them. The world was their game board and Dad moved the pieces. Their approach to sex was provocative and international in attitude, and scope. They did not have the luxury of living a quiet, settled life together. Emma and Dad established an agreement early on in their relationship. Theirs was an arrangement some people could never understand or accept.

love's symphony

my poetry
is set to music
as I scream
his name into the wind

In his mind, then in an outline on paper, Mitch summarized what he discovered in his reading.

"Only a year after Dad and Emma met, she dropped out of school for two semesters to work. To be near him, she stayed around the little college town in her own apartment. It was a difficult time for her. She worked hard and saved enough money to return to school and her studies.

In the summer of the following year, Emma finally went back to her course work. With very little support from home, she obtained student loans through a local bank and worked her way through school. Dad helped her, when he could.

In college, at the undergraduate level, Emma majored in studio art and European history. Only five art historians taught at the small university's art department so she took Luke's art history classes for something like three years. She also worked in the art department and in the visual resources library.

Her senior year, she became Luke's teaching assistant. No one was aware Emma and Luke had anything but a student-mentor relationship. Emma obtained the equivalent of a third major, in art history, although the university did not offer a major in that course of study at that time. She graduated with three majors.

After she returned from Europe, she attended graduate school in another state, she majored in art history but hung out at the library and the writing center. She completed her course work in a year and a half. Her best intellectual gifts were research, analyzing data, and writing. When Emma was ready to graduate, Luke wrote references for her. He helped her decide which PhD program to enter.

During those years, Dad was her adviser and her lover. Eventually, he grew to be her only family. They organized their households and families around their love and established a way of life that worked for them."

no morning coffee

he strode away
from the warmth of my bed
readied himself
and was absorbed
into the cold of the morning

I caress the sheets now
in the same way I caress him

Nude, I stretch
and attain the full length
of the bed

I lie here
luxuriating
in the warmth
that he left

and
I created

gate

then caught in the sway of time
I move toward the moments
I knew him
when our existences touched
when I heard his voice

I still hear…
no I must not speak the obvious
time for us was instants   they just were
it was   it just was
time is no beginning
except at the wedding
of time our father and earth our mother
when then   they united like us
and we began

Emma and Dave

After Mitchell came to Luke and Angela, Luke's wife, they had Mitchell to raise.

Emma and Luke continued their affair. Nevertheless, Emma began a relationship with a undergraduate student in her senior year. Dave was his name. He was in college ROTC. When he graduated, the army commissioned him an army officer.

She met Dave when he was twenty. She was two years older. Not many students outside the ROTC (Reserved Officer Training Corp) department knew him. He majored in art education. He took an art appreciation class rather than art history courses. He wasn't the typical art major.

Emma and Dave met in one of the studio art classes. He was nerdy and he was not in sync with what was going on. He decided to pursue Emma when she defended him during a political argument in a class they both attended.

He followed her around like a puppy. Only after she gave him a complete makeover from head to toe, did she agree to date him. She helped him with his clothes and his hair, with his style. During their early relationship, she placed no ties on Dave, nor did he place any on her.

She told Luke all about the makeover. Luke found it amusing and proposed doing a little sex makeover with Dave, too. Although he was never the lover that Luke was and sometimes didn't respond, Emma attempted to educate Dave sexually with advanced instruction from Luke.

Some weekends, Emma had an hour or two with Dave then she would meet Luke a few hours later. Emma's dates with Dave enhanced her lovemaking with Luke.

The knowledge she was just with someone else drove Luke wild. He liked the competition. His pleasure in the game was enormous.

All of the young women Emma knew had their date and sex stories, she possessed the ultimate story but she told no one. It was all part of the adventure for Emma and she loved it.

Occasionally, Luke was required to play the dutiful husband to Angela, but Emma never asked to hear about it. Angela had very little time for Luke. She wouldn't listen to Luke about sex. She made love only in the missionary position, did nothing oral, and believed sex was boring for the woman. Emma wrote, "I find the entire thing between them terribly dull. Angela was too busy with her addictions and her complaints about Luke to enjoy sex, or life."

As for Dave, his numbers went up tremendously when he started dating Emma. His campus life changed. Emma brought advantages to Dave that followed him throughout his life.

After Luke realized it was impossible for him to divorce Angela, he suggested to Emma that she marry **young Dave**.

"Why not?" Luke wrote Emma.

"He has a reasonably good future. The situation is near perfect. The important thing is the travel in Europe, and around the world. You can see in reality what I could only show you on the classroom screens. If you marry him, a good future may be yours. You can polish your language skills and develop your cultural sense. After you return from Europe, you can attend a PhD program, graduate, teach."

Luke always called Dave, the guy. Emma married him just after he graduated from college. Luke went to the wedding. It was small but elegant with only close friends and relatives in attendance.

He finally met the mother that produced his wonderful lover. He found her toxic, to say the least, and wondered if Emma were actually related to her. Her mother spent the evening pointing out what she thought was wrong with everything concerning the wedding.

Emma wore a princess-cut, cream color dress. Dave wore his dress blues. He was dashing and she was stunning.

Mitchell picked up the laminated newspaper photo of Emma and Dave's wedding and examined it closely. He found his dad in the photo. He saw a much younger man than Mitch remembered. His Dad sat in the second pew to her right behind Emma.

Mitch thought sweet Emma. She looks so good, so proud, and ready for what life had to offer. Why are relationships so damn difficult.

Luke wrote he cried at the wedding. He only cried three times in his adult life. Emma's wedding was one of them. According to his journal entry in the file, Luke was never involved with a student again. By the time Emma left with Dave, he had a career to consider and a son to raise.

For his son's future, Luke stayed where he was at the university and remained with Angela in an unhappy marriage. He continued with his life, such as it was, and with his profession. He lived vicariously through Emma.

In Luke's mind, he was committed to Emma on some level that defied physical existence and time and space. Husbands and lovers made no difference to him.

"Emma wrote something which says so much about **the rest of her** life, Dad." Mitch realized he was talking to his dead father. He didn't care. Mitch opened the paper and began to read aloud. His voice echoed through their house:

suppose
our world was new
and there was no
dying

then I could
love you
once more
and there would
be no
end

if ever
the world
is new
again
and there is
only
living

I hope we
meet
somewhere
and share

time
without
end

Mitch whispered, "Emma wrote the poem when she was still in college."

Husband

In college, Emma's husband majored in art education. He never taught and he never used his major. He would rarely talk to Emma about art or history. In fact, he rarely talked at all.

Emma would have suffocated in that environment if she had not traveled and experienced life. For a while, during his first assignment in Europe, Dave traveled with her. Later, his promotion and military responsibilities took him away from her, their home, and their marriage.

She could have spent her entire marriage waiting for him. He was often away on some temporary duty, TDY, assignment. Even when he was in the area, he was rarely around. When he was at home, his thoughts were still at the company or battalion headquarters. If Dave were going to continue in a military career, neither of them had a choice. She was on her own.

They went their separate ways and Dave had his casual affairs.

Because of her husband's rank, Emma was required to **participate** in army community activities and volunteer much of her time. Officers were the equivalent of upper level managers in the civilian world

For someone who strove to be an intellectual, the environment became stifling. Emma decided to continue to travel' alone, or so her husband thought. Her free verse tells the story of a trip she made to North Africa:

Yes, I went there
to the Sahara
looking for a mirage and a lover
that turned out to be both

the desert was extraordinary

the earth
even in its despair
can produce incredible beauty
when the heat of day
gives way to cool night
the oasis of date palms and spring water
turns into a sensuous jasmine-filled dream

Yes, I traveled the Sahara
with sand roses
Bedouin drums
Fatima's hand and desert heat
scooping sand with my sandals
walking through Roman ruins
reading French signs
"*buvez coca-cola*"
and creating a *mirage*

In her **journal entry**, Emma described in detail the *Bedouin* wedding she watched in the Sahara. After the ceremony, the continual, nightlong rhythm of the drums was sensuous. The perfume of jasmine filled the desert air and wafted around the date palms.

Her lover appeared out of the desert night and stood beside her on her balcony while the drums beat. He leaned in toward her, close to her ear and whispered, "The rhythm is almost overwhelming, no?"

He slipped behind her and began to move to the sounds of the drums. Apparently, their night of passion was incredible. It was one of Luke's favorite stories.

According to Luke, he took pleasure in Emma's sexual exploits and encouraged her to write about them. Wherever Emma and Luke met, her stories were a prelude to their lovemaking.

Emma delighted in every moment she spent in Europe and documented her adventures in her journals, other writings, and her letters to Luke. She drew upon those memories in later years, when things were much different for her. All these events occurred before 2001.

Tunisia

We walked in the most stunning of turquoise and white settings on a hill that ran along the edge of the Mediterranean and the northern shores of Africa.

We just arrived in *Sidi Bou Said* at a restaurant that faced the sea. Below us, stood the ruins of the ancient Phoenician city *Cartago.* A modern marina floated to the left. All the creamy white dwellings were covered with the lavender color of wisteria that climbed every wall. Their scent filled the air.

My lover who was also my guide accompanied me. Oh, don't be surprised everything I did and touched in that place at that time was something disallowed. I indulged myself with the forbidden. My entire North African excursion was wonderful, except ...

We met my lover's brother and his British girlfriend for luncheon.

I sat at the dining table across from the brother, an employee at the American embassy, who announced while he nodded in the general direction of the embassy "I hate all those fat pig men over there."

He was Tunisian. The pig men were American. I was shocked, at first, distracted. Then alarm bells went off in my head.

The timeline was nowhere near Arab Spring 2011 or even 9/11/01 but I knew something astounding was just proclaimed in that luncheon conversation in such a beautiful location. In front of me was a world I relished, savored, romanticized but did not comprehend.

Much later I realized I was privy to the darkest of forewarnings.

predictable in retrospect

when a riddler strips himself
and mounts the scaffold
he calls no-regrets

courageous before all humans
he dares not describe himself
as dangling on a gallows
or suspended on a tree-of-life bough

in stormy crosswinds near a cliff
he challenges spectators
to guess his identity
just as a Gallic cross appears
near the Spin Ghar mountains
Khyber-pass-perpendicularity

the fiddler asks who profits
from the games of Armageddon and
words doused with gasoline
mediums doused with psychosis
and earth doused

with someone's no-regrets

map

I'll follow the wind
down the winding path
dream unfettered
liberated   shaking
but this doesn't resemble the road
I knew in my last quarters
this route looks unfamiliar
        more like a roller coaster

nonetheless indications are
well   I'm untraceable
they're clueless   always were
I'm off the grid
file the flight plan
        try Madrid

Emma's mail to Luke arrived from everywhere, all over Europe, Africa, and Asia, especially Japan. She went to the Tokyo museum, just because she knew Luke loved the Edo period.

She visited archeological sites worldwide. She was particularly fond of the sites in North Africa where the Roman Empire built their colonial cities. In Europe, she walked the remnants of a wall called the *Limes,* the original Iron Curtain. Her curiosity engaged, Emma began to research the reasons for the wall.

She visited most of the European cathedrals and major museums. She observed holidays in different areas of the world. Emma spent a Christmas Day in Westminster Abbey, London, New Year's Eve in Sydney, the end of Ramadan in *Sidi Bou Said*, Easter in the *Notre Dame de Paris*, Orthodox Easter week in Athens, May Day in Lisbon, and celebrated in Barcelona for the hell of it.

She encamped at a Lake Como villa with her Swiss lover in the summers. René introduced her to an international set of players. He provided her with almost anything she wanted. He was married, so, of course, René also gave Emma freedom to explore her world.

Mitch sat in his chair chuckling at the list his father compiled. "Look at these names! Dad entitled it Liaisons." She met some of the most surprising people. "Emma pretty much travelled every continent. This is amazing."

On the back of an Italian post card displaying a Venetian sunrise, Emma wrote:

Venice
at sunrise
is the tangible
afterglow
of all night
lovemaking

mmmmmm
wish you were here

She made no apologies.

"Emma addressed the post card to Dad and sent it to him at his university P.O. Box in an envelope. Guess Angela wouldn't have approved of their corresponding."

Mitch never called Angela mother and she never insisted.

uninterrupted

some say love lasts forever
but forever is relative

I’ve known minutes
that were forever

I can still
feel them

where is he
I keep remembering

Emma reclined on a private beach **near Cannes**. Her breasts were bare to the sun. She heard or felt some movement close to her. She turned her head.

The figure silhouetted by the glare off the white sand and the turquoise water turned toward her. The fantasy she carried with her, everywhere she traveled, had come true.

She heard his voice before her eyes could focus on him. Luke's face slowly materialized in her field of vision as he moved out of the sunlight and into the shade of the canopy. They didn't say a word.

He scooped the container of lotion off the low table and walked over to her. He knelt down and slowly rubbed the lotion into her stomach. His hands moved to her thighs and he messaged the lotion around the little triangle of her bikini. He moved down her legs lifting one and the other as he applied the cream. Luke rubbed it into her feet and toes moving up and down on each toe with his cupped hand and his fingers.

He kneeled and for a good two minutes, he messaged both of her insteps. While he was on his knees, he wiped his hands with one of the towels and reapplied the lotion to her stomach.

While he did all this, he stared at her nipples. He imagined his mouth on them. Their musky taste filled his mind. Instead of tasting them, he poured more lotion into his hands and rubbed them.
Her nipples tightened. He pulled at them. As tight as they were, they hardened more in his fingertips. She moaned. He was also hard.

Emma's excitement was fueled by the sounds that the lotion made in his hands. They sounded like sex and it excited her. His touch was so sensual every molecule on Emma's skin was in a heightened state of arousal.

He bent over her and started kissing her ears. He sucked her ear lobes as if they were her nipples. His mouth moved to hers. She sucked his tongue as if it were his penis.

She stood up and took him by the hand. She led him into the striped beach tent and gestured to the large, soft towels and pillows on the chaise. He scattered them around the floor.

Luke lay down and pulled his trunks off. He motioned to her and she straddled him planting her feet at his sides. Emma lowered herself down toward his penis. She pulled her thong to the side. She held his erection in her hand and slowly took him inside. The feel of him was exquisite.

As she crouched over his body, she moved up and down on him. He thrust back with all he had. They attempted to quench a desire that burned during the months they lived without each other. Their sex was hard and furious. Their arousal was extreme.

"Mmmm, ohhhh god," he looked up at the one thing in the world that drove him out of his mind, that made him do things like invent symposiums and conferences to attend, and caused him to fly a few thousand miles just to touch.

They did not speak for over thirty minutes because they didn't want to break the splendid, heady spell of the moment. They reveled in the touch of one another after such a long separation. At length, the waves breaking on the beach lulled them. She snuggled into his side and they fell asleep.

When they woke, the sun was setting over the Mediterranean. They stood facing the sea. He looked at her, "if there is something better than this, I don't know what it is."

"Can we stay here forever? Yes, say yes, Luke."

"In six weeks, we'll see each other again in Copenhagen."

treatise ancien

and the midnight moon weaves
a bright necklace through the deep
whose vast expanse gently heaves
as an immortal asleep

so this spirit bows before you
with a full but soft emotion
like the swell of summers' oceans
in gaiety and glee

we will capture the splendor of these waves
grave wounds and forlorn hopes forgotten

no feigned love   no scowls
we will discern the breadth
and depth of our devotion

we will treasure dark and light

who holds freedom
and what is free

Later **at dinner**, Emma sighed, "within the coming year, Dave will be re-assigned. In a few months, we have to say good-bye to Europe for a while. I'm glad you and I could meet here. I can't wait to see you in Denmark, and eventually in the States."

She looked down into her plate and lightly stabbed at her food with her fork. She looked up at Luke. "I guess it's a good thing I married someone with the profession and resources Dave has, but the marriage is difficult, Luke. I don't know if it's going to work. He's not at home much. He's so cold. He doesn't even like to kiss anymore!"

She had never complained to him about her marriage. Luke gave her a momentary look. He understood. He couldn't stand her husband either.

Just to lighten her mood, he half mischievously and half seriously remarked, "You've made your own advantages, and you know it. Your circumstances do not depend on him. Ignore him."

She smiled, then laughed. Shaking her head yes.

He leaned toward her and with a lowered voice, "I've taught you well. I am proud of you. Don't let him get to you. What will you do about René?"

"I haven't even told René!"

"He will miss you. I'm sure of it. He loves you, too. He is someone you don't want to lose, Emma. Make him a lifelong friend, if not a lifelong lover."

Lake Como

feeling evening coming
sunshine paling
shadows lengthening
a hush falling
softening day into dusk

star shines silently
moon lights brightly
footsteps softly
from long ago

Part IV
Children

homecoming

When my first daughter was born in Michigan near an air base, the weather was cold for June. In May, I planted flowers and groundcover in the little plot of broken ground in the front of our quarters. I also rejuvenated the red rose bush by the door.

Dave left me there to unpack, I was almost eight months pregnant and he left for temporary duty somewhere in Georgia or Virginia or Alabama. I settled into quarters all alone. While he was gone, I unpacked, bought furniture, laid carpet remnants, gardened, mowed grass. I knew no one there so I stayed busy around our quarters.

While I watered, trimmed and fertilized the rose bush, I talked to it or I mean to her. I told her everything because she reminded me of my grandmother whom I adored. My grandmother won prizes with her rose bushes.

Other than the baby in my stomach, the rose bush was all I had to talk to. I wondered aloud to her about the timing of the baby's arrival and if my husband would be there for the birth. I didn't want to deliver a child alone.

Dave returned a month after Isabel was born.

I don't know how **the rose** bush did it but I knew, I sensed, the baby would be healthy, a normal weight, and a girl. She was born the same day that the first bud on the rose bush bloomed.

vessel

this blossom   this flower
this rose   reflector of feelings
narrator for a shy lover
symbol of friendship and respect
creator of memories
scented lifter of spirits
honored guest at many festivities
fête joie   gaieté   merriment
colorful perpetuator of gracious deeds
swift Proserpine
rower of the boat that embarks
for the romance island Cythera

punch line   compassionate soother of the unwell
and the mourning,
acknowledger of patriarchal and matriarchal love
mender of broken promises
and a guide for broken hearts

appears at my doorstep

to conduct a conversation with me

lacustrine

I've spent life
in a perfect day
doing nothing

enjoying
the sounds of the earth
the golden sunshine
the sweet laughter of children

sensuous heat
still and narcotic
invading my body

lulling me
caressing me with calm

oh
summer linger here
and go
with me
when I leave

I love
the air
that I breathe

PIVOT

I began rubbing my belly and he joined in. "I'm proud of myself for getting pregnant so easily for the second time in my thirties."

My stomach was just a little round. I looked at him and he began kissing me. His hands felt good. They moved to my hips. He pulled me to him.

"Sexy."

We kissed, again. In that moment, both of us realized we were too tired to make love.

He chuckled, "this is pitiful. We have to get some rest." He rolled over on his back. His eyes half closed.

I reached for the cocoa butter on the bedside table and resumed rubbing my stomach. My darling little Kathryn grew in my stomach.

By the time she was three and Isabel was five, we were thousands of miles away from Dave. I was a working, single mother. We were on our own.

what draws this image

to paint a hopeful picture
in a stone and white clapboard house in Maryland
or an abandoned service station in San Jose
a flooded New Orleans
or in a frosty mug of root beer outside Tucson
is a confident gesture

but we're moving away from the topic
I love to drift

cabbage can withstand frost
I've been told
in sunshine
in a rainy day
after midnight
in quixotic weather
or the dawn hours that poets adore
faith in one's self should withstand
high altitudes or others' negative outlooks

who paints a buoyant picture in a Peruvian
emerald mine   who asks for positive reflection
in a deep dark enclosure while digging for
precious stones   a prayer to a deity
any deity   can drift skyward

I hold the night in my hands
and paint it with a deep cobalt blue

Following her international adventures, Emma created stability and a relative amount of comfort in her life with her husband. During that time, she lost one of her true and absolute loves, art history. Only to have love returned to her in another way by one of her children.

The children changed everything. Emma wrote sporadically after they were born. She was very busy with them. They were born only 22 months apart. The birth of her first daughter, Emma Isabel, was a happy occasion, except the in-laws were disappointed the child wasn't a boy. They never thought to be thankful the baby was healthy. It was just expected Emma would have a healthy child.

Then a second daughter, Emma Kathryn, was born. Emma was pleased that Dave didn't mind that the first name of each child was Emma. She didn't realize her husband wasn't concerned about the children's names. He wanted a son. Emma's father-in-law cried when Dave told him the second child wasn't a boy.

When the children were very young, encouraged by his parents, Dave already had one foot out the door. Emma's husband was disinterested in his family. The young man Emma met in college and thought would be a stable, secure force in her life turned out to be anything but.

Kathryn was born with *miconium illeus* and edema and was almost a month late. Emma's Ob-gyn tried to induce birth earlier in the month, but the procedure had not worked, he left for Hawaii. Neither, she or the baby received treatment or tests during this critical stage in her pregnancy. The attending OB/GYN followed the dictates that the child should take precedent over the mother.

Following her delivery, the attendants wrapped Emma in warm blankets and left. She shook for what seemed like hours alone.

After her stay in the recovery room, staff pushed Emma's bed into a private room, and left her there. No one brought the baby to her. Dave disappeared. No medical staff came in to help her clean up. She fell asleep. Someone came in to the room, shook her, and told her that she should go to the nursery.

Emma walked down the hospital corridor alone. She held her still puffy belly as she walked because she felt like her insides were coming out. No one helped her. She didn't see a wheelchair anywhere. She rounded the corner to the left and saw the nursery window. Three babies lay in bassinets.

Kathryn was completely nude and lying under heat lights to the right of the other babies in a separate room. A nun dressed all in black stood over her administering last rites.

Emma was admitted to a hospital only one other time in her life and that was when Isabel was born. Last rites and medical procedures weren't familiar to her. She could tell you the history of the church and the beautiful art and architecture produced by Catholicism but had no personal experience with specific ceremonies. The scene before Emma looked bizarre to her.

One of the nursery attendants walked through the nursery door, she told Emma, "that's the last rites," then returned to the room.

Emma repeated over and over " nooo, nooo!" She stood in the nursery in a bloody hospital gown with no one around to talk to or comfort her.

Except for back labor, Isabel's birth had been almost effortless for Emma. Kathryn's birth was so difficult. She wasn't given time to recuperate. Emma was small and the delivery was hard on her body. The baby was edemic. Kathryn's little swollen body weighed over ten pounds.

Within the first forty hours of her life, an ambulance rushed Kathryn to neonatal surgery in a children's hospital far from the hospital where she was born. Dave did not go with his child but showed up at the hospital later. No one was there when the surgeon removed a small section of the baby's intestines and vacuumed the rest.

Little Kathryn was diagnosed with cystic fibrosis.

While the baby was in neonatal intensive care, geneticists at the children's hospital filled Dave with mostly negative information and fear. He didn't possess the psychological make-up to deal with that kind of bad news. They gave him a couple of pamphlets. He left the meeting with them.

Dave gritted his teeth the entire time the baby was in the neonatal ICU. He told himself he was not going to live a life that required taking care of a sick child. He did not like children much, anyway. His mother wanted to be a grandmother. His parents wanted someone to carry the family name. He gave himself excuses and gave little help or solace to Emma.

The next day, after Dave told Emma about the baby's diagnosis, he handed her one of the pamphlets the geneticists gave him. He did not say much more. He could not speak the words.

Clutching her stomach and the pain inside it, Emma got out of her hospital bed and drove with Dave to the children's hospital. She walked a long way, through parking lots, entrances, and corridors, unaided, to her baby's hospital crib. She was not concerned about her own health but she should have been.

During Emma's lifetime, she would spend many weeks beside Kathryn's bed in one hospital or another reading the latest, updated information about cystic fibrosis. The information never mentioned a cure or real hope at all.

In the pamphlet Dave placed in her hand, Emma read that Kathryn would have digestive and breathing problems all her life. The pamphlet stated the disease was centered in the pancreas and lungs. The disease was hereditary, and both parents carried the gene.

While Kathryn was in the hospital, Dave's mother took care of Isabel and that worried Emma. She was concerned about the woman's influence on her little girl.

Dave's parents' reaction to Kathryn's diagnosis was denial. For years, if Emma tried to discuss Kathryn's illness with them, a comment like 'ahh, there's nothing wrong with the child,' was what she heard.

A hurt descended on Emma that she couldn't escape for years. Her feelings remained hidden because she was determined not to display sorrow to the children, to the dysfunctional families on both sides of her children's family tree, or to the world in general. She was not going to let this defeat her or claim her little family.

Dave walked away before Kathryn was three years old. He said her illness would hurt his career. He just wanted an excuse. Emma always thought of his selfish acts as a Dave-style retribution for his very apparent shortcomings that he blamed on everyone but himself.

In retribution for having a family ruin his plans, he harmed his child in the most despicable way. Kathryn toddled into the kitchen and told Emma what happened. Emma dropped to her knees, held her daughter and sobbed.

She was afraid of her own emotions. Not only was her mother a huge disappointment, but now Dave was a disgusting bastard. She abhorred him.

Dave was a military man, but a coward when he had to defend his wife to his parents or care for an ill child. Emma and her babies lost their home. They were left to fend for themselves.

Mitch looked up from the papers. "What was up with that damn hospital and that son of a bitch...this is horrible!"

He had not heard the story surrounding Kathryn's birth and early life before.

Emma was too embarrassed and hesitant to tell Luke when Dave walked away. She was afraid of what Luke would do. She did not talk or correspond with them during this **unsettled** part of her life, but Luke and Mitch always remained in her thoughts.

Although she earned two master's degrees and was ABD in her PHD course work from top-rated universities, she only found an adjunct position in 'an ill-managed, little community college/education corporation.'

The school was located in a city near a military facility. The children were still military dependents so the post provided medical care and other benefits for both her daughters. Emma had child support from Dave and combined with an erratic salary from adjunct teaching, she was able to buy a house. Only then, did she contact Luke and tell him what happened.

terrain and time

I've sighed like winds through coastal canyons
I've flowed backward like a river during
a heaving earthquake
I've crushed mountains trying
to protect my own
I've clashed like crashing fault lines
I've formed reservoirs in deep crevices of
split terrain
I've cried lakes-full during life's sorrows
I've thundered like towering black storm
clouds
I've bent like grains in drenching downpours

I've absorbed disparagement
like the moon's surface sops up meteor blows

I've formed into clouds
shifted in front of the sun
dappled the landscape with shadow
and
I've born the sublime

One day, Luke came to them. Mitch attended summer camp and Luke took **two weeks off**. He told Angela he was leaving for an archeology dig site to complete research for a paper he was writing. The site was located on a small Greek island and it was impossible to contact him.

Emma stood at the front door waiting for Luke when he pulled up. He picked her up in his arms on the porch of the craftsman cottage where she and the children lived. Luke covered Emma with kisses. Emma's children were standing near her, following his every move. He looked down at them and then back at Emma, "Not like the old days, huh." They laughed.

Luke scooped Isabel into his arms. He asked her, "How's my waskally wabbit?"

"Fi-i-nne," Isabel reached up to touch his face. Her mouth was open.

Emma picked-up Kathryn and away they went into the house. For those two weeks, Emma was happier than she imagined one person, just less a family, could be. When Luke left, the good-byes were difficult. It had been a glorious two weeks. Both children already called him Daddy Luke. The girls were aged four and six at the time.

Luke drove to Mitch's summer camp with a heavy heart. He wanted to turn his car around and drive Mitch back to Emma, to his true family.

He asked himself, "How would I support them?" He knew the answer before he posed the question, "I couldn't. If I do this, I will lose my position at the university, I will lose tenure."

Instead of returning to where his heart wanted him to go and after picking-up Mitch at camp, Luke turned his car in the direction of the university town.

While he visited with them, Luke and Emma made **plans** concerning their future. Their goals were set and they pledged to each other that somehow, some day, they would unite their children under one roof.

Luke urged Emma to continue to keep her mother at bay and away from the children. Emma told him how her mother organized, what the kids called, ambush visits. She would just show up.

Emma's mother would attempt to pick fights with her and criticize Emma in front of her children. The air in the house would fill with her venom and cigarette smoke. She never considered Kathryn's breathing problems. She told Isabel who seemed dissatisfied with her circumstances at times, that she could always 'come live with me.'

Luke pled, "I have such a bad feeling about your mother. Emma, do not allow her to insinuate herself further into their lives. Do not allow her to disrupt their home life or poison these sweet children. Please."

During those years, Emma managed her **family**'s lives as best she could, but it was difficult for her. Everything in Emma's life devolved. She reflected on the adventures she had as a young woman in her twenties and early thirties. She wrote about them in her poems and short stories:

"Sometimes life leads you down paths you thought you would never take. This happened to me the night my second child, Kathryn, was born. Kathryn taught me so much. She taught me humility and patience. The love I received from her eclipsed the other loves in my life.

I could never be the beautiful person inside that she was. She smiled at me and gave me strength when I thought I could not go on. Sadness sometimes overwhelmed me, she sensed my mood and tried to make me laugh.

I still remember her first laugh as a baby. Her eyes twinkled with delight. Her intelligence shone bright in her eyes. I took a step back and look at her twice. I asked myself, is this really my child? She embraced life with courage and wisdom. She was charming, endearing, funny, and warm.

When she was a girl, her honey-color long hair cascaded down her back. She won everyone over with her smile. Her eyes were a dark green, big, and inquisitive. She observed everything about the earth and humans, taking it all in.

She taught herself to read at four. Even at the age of four, she displayed wisdom and thoughtfulness. I always thought she was an old soul.

She bore pain with such dignity and will. No matter what the various hospitals dished out, she took it. As she grew, Kathryn learned medical procedures so she could follow and understand the doctors and nurses' treatments and other processes concerning her health.

She had a PDR (Physicians' Desk Reference) when she was ten years old. She tried to teach herself Latin. She studied Grey's Anatomy, an anatomy book for medical students. With her knowledge, she caught several potentially deadly mistakes that saved her life in the course of her treatments.

I watched her learn and mature, I realized all things are temporary. All we really have as human beings are love and memories. Life gives us pain and suffering. If we deal with those burdens with dignity, it makes all the difference.

Her older sister, Isabel, was smart but not in the same way. There was an untamed side to her that always kept Kathryn and me a little on edge. Isabel's big, dark, expressive eyes and long brunette hair matched her bold, fearless personality. She was very determined when she made up her mind to do something and sometimes she turned too aggressive. Kathryn learned to keep her in check, though. It was a glorious thing to observe.

I recognize Kathryn sounds like a child too good to be true. Some of the medical professionals around us told me that children with cystic fibrosis generally have these traits. A lot of them are artistic and intelligent. All these traits align in the same area of the human genome where the CF gene occurs.

Children with cystic fibrosis also possess patience and a tremendous capacity for forgiveness. Sometimes people around children with CF say and do such inappropriate things. The children's capacity for forgiveness helps with their survival from day to day.

children
dans ma vie, j'ai choisi

I have life
growing around me
and a home full of love

I drive to a college
full of theories
dead space
thick air

I hear words
no longer applicable
to the living
of my days

they pretend
and I tend
to life

in my life
I chose

I will
always
choose love

the snake

I was inside my house near the creek grading papers one day comfortable in the knowledge that my children were outside playing within the fenced backyard.

Just as I finished the first class's work my youngest daughter ran screaming into the house, something awoke my mama bear instincts

"What, what's going on baby."

She announced as loud as a four year old could scream that a snake danced in front of her then slithered under the gate. I grabbed the key to the gate and because I knew the snake might return, I seized a garden hoe that stood on the backyard patio.

Through the gate I saw the snake midway into the side yard that separated my house from the creek. The snake stopped turned around and stood up about a foot off the ground, bobbing and hissing, it challenged me.

Before I could really think, I moved to a position in front of the snake and lifted the sharp hoe. Down it came on the snake's head. I severed it from the snake's body. Not knowing whether snakes were similar to fishing worms, I cut the snake in several more pieces, just in case.

All this happened in front of my two daughters who stood behind me with their hands over their mouths. They returned to the backyard where they sat in the sandbox while I cleaned up 'the mess.'

They were deep in conversation when I walked over to them at the end of what I thought was the resolution of the snake problem. They stared at me for what seemed like a full minute, then they said in unison "poor snake."

For a couple of weeks after the snake episode I received sidelong glances, raised eyebrows and whispers.

One weekend in the kitchen, I flashed on an episode in my own childhood that led me to understand what the children were doing and experiencing. It was that chicken again.

When a child witnesses adults exercise their powers over life and death they become anxious. They don't really understand the capabilities of the people they're living with. In some cultures, the killing might simply mean a meal, or a ritual sacrifice, or both. Perhaps most children witness adults kill something and somewhere deep inside them think they might be next.

Select

good flows
through
this universe
of human souls
as a babbling
spring
flows
through
the desert
and with
as much welcome

School

The teachers could not comprehend Kathryn's illness so they didn't treat her well. Sometimes, the teachers' behavior was inadvertent, sometimes not.

When I found another adjunct position, I commuted to a town across the state line to teach at a university there. The commute made it difficult for me to go to their school during the workday. Still, I went to Kathryn and Isabel's school many times to talk to their teachers about one thing or another.

My children were bored in school. Isabel attended gifted and talented classes. Kathryn was way ahead of her classmates. Her teacher said she "asked too many questions." They were too much for the local educational system. I decided to home school them after talking to their military pediatrician. My choice meant another change in our lives.

Unlike the schools, I did not put into place or allow philosophical, religious, or psychological barriers to block their learning. I only challenged them to acquire knowledge. They both tested in the top 4th percentile in the country. I believe their scores were the result of their freedom to speak without constraint and to learn at their own pace. And, gender wasn't an issue in their learning.

Kathryn tried to take in the physical and human world as quickly as she could. She did not have the time most people have. Perhaps she sensed this, I will never know. Her **prognosis** was given to me at birth. It weighed heavily on me.

If her teachers had read the information about cystic fibrosis I handed to them or recalled some of their training as teachers, there might not have been a problem.

Except for the times when I was exhausted from teaching my children and still had a million things to do around the house, I never regretted home schooling them. Well, almost never.

When Isabel was older, she saw in me, and me alone, all of the points of rebellion other teenagers see in a lot of things in their lives. Their rebellious nature facilitates their leaving home which Isabel did prematurely, to marry too soon.

I understand, though. I only wish I handled it better.

a change of weather

the rumble of thunder
can be heard
out there on the horizon
that is changing
from gray to grayer

an Autumn wind is blowing
across the landscape
across time
through my window
and across my table

a thieving cold tempest
will shake the trees
and deprive them
of their leaves
and me of the green
that my senses depend upon

the gusty rumble brings
a winter wind to my gate
bare trees to my eyes
and a chill to this house

this wind bears a frosting
that penetrates
way down past the bone

the wind brings a predator
that will bare skin and soul
and leave you to contemplate
the death that marauds
through winter

reverberating

I phoned Luke. I knew his wife was in the hospital again. I would be lucky if I caught him at **home**. Mitch answered the phone. My dear, sweet Mitch, I loved him. He had been a precious little boy. However, he was difficult as a teenager. After he grew older, I could not talk to him. Because of Angela, he went through a lot. I truly wish I could have helped him more.

He and Isabel were a lot alike. I would not say that to Isabel because she did not like Mitch.

During this particular phone call, he talked to me. "Hello, Mitch, how are you doing?"

"Fine," he replied. He lowered his voice. I could feel his frustration.

I told him, "This is difficult time for you. Hang in there. It will get better. One day, you'll be out on your own, you'll have your own life and family..."

Mitch interrupted me. He spoke very quietly.

"I think Dad is exhausted. He's teaching, going to the hospital to see Angela, and then taking a little time to be with me. We just finished a late breakfast. He's not eating much."

He sighed. "Angela is always causing problems, even when she's sick."

"I'm sorry, Mitch. Just help your dad as much as possible--he needs you right now."

"Dad'll be glad, to hear your voice."

"I'll get him."

He did not go get him. He yelled, "Daaddddd, phooonnnne."

Luke and I had not communicated by phone for a two weeks. We followed the events in each other's lives by email. On various holidays, birthdays and anniversaries, we sent greeting cards.

When we talked on the phone, we spent hours discussing our everyday lives. We compared notes on teaching, on running a household alone, on our children.

Luke delighted in hearing stories about the children. He was concerned about Kathryn's health. He was concerned about how it affected our little family. He was always interested in Isabel. He was proud of them and approved of their home schooling.

He made suggestions about what I should teach them. His ideas about their education emphasized survival skills and the how-tos of life along with the academic subjects.

“Teach them about their financial lives. Show them how to make and manage money, how to function at their best in everyday life, how to survive emergencies, and how to defend themselves.”

We usually discussed vague plans about meeting somewhere. First, Kathryn was hospitalized. Then, Luke’s wife, Angela, was hospitalized. We postponed our visits with each other on a regular basis. We laughed about it after a while.

"Luke, how are you, Sweetheart."

"Emma!"

"Emma, my love, how good of you to call." Luke’s baritone voice was strong and precise, yet melodic. This came from years of earning his living with his speech. It gave me cold chill bumps to hear it, always.

Instantly, his voice transported me back to his darkened classroom, his arms wrapped around me, and his voice whispering in my ear. We were both older, but the bond was still there and always would be. I was as certain of it as he was.

"How is Angela?"

"Not well--I'm going to bring her home for a while, though, see how it goes. If it goes badly, I may have to place her in an extended care facility. The next step will be a hospice. Her physicians recommended I do so."

"Sorry to hear it." I hesitated, "but, Mitch will be better off without her there in your home. I wish that weren't the truth."

"It's okay." Luke added, "All these years, I thought it would work, start working, at some point."

"Luke, is Mitch near you?"

"Yes, in the next room."

"Then, we can't say much right now. Know this, I love you and my thoughts are with you both."

"There are tears in my eyes as we speak because I miss you so much."

I paused and swallowed hard so I could go on. "You didn't tell me about you. How are you?"

"I would be lying if I told you I'm all right. I'm exhausted and very concerned about things."

"I understand. I shouldn't bother you about why I called, then."

"It's alright, tell me."

"Oh, Luke, Kathryn's health..."

"I know, my Love. I know."

"She wants to do something. The project will keep her, and Isabel, occupied and it will help with the home schooling. Isabel is excited about helping her sister with this. She would like the information, too."

"Two questions, what is the information they want and how is my Isabel?"

"Isabel is a handful, as usual. She is growing, of course, and healthy. She wants to talk to you. They are both here. They just came into the room. I'll put them on the speakerphone."

"Hiiiiii, Daddy Luke," They said in unison.

"Hiii, guys! What's up?"

Kathryn said, "We, we want to, well..."

Isabel interrupted her, "we want to find out about our ancestors. Kathryn wants to tell their history, she wants to meet a European, a northern one...and what else, oh yea, she wants to know how long people have known about CF and what its origins are."

"Whoa, that's a lot of research."

"We know." Kathryn declared.

Isabel asked, "Will you help us?"

Luke could have said he was busy but he didn't. "I'll try."

"Yeaaay!" The kids started jumping up and down. "Thank you. Thank you!"

"Isabel, be good, and mind your Mom, okay. Kathryn, take real good care of yourself. We will talk about this project on the phone next week. I can give you some information then. I will call you Wednesday evening. Now put your Mom on the phone. Love ya."

"Byyyye. We love you. "

Isabel walked into the living room mumbling, "He's always telling me to be good."

Kathryn followed her, "well, somebody needs to."

Mitch again

When Angela was dying of cancer and needed constant attention, Luke could not be with Emma as much as he would have liked.

During that time in their lives, their contact consisted mostly of phone calls and letters. Luke and Emma tried to keep each other going. Their long distance relationship was difficult. Still, Luke and Emma were thankful for each other.

Emma encouraged Luke to keep going with his teaching and research. She reminded him that he was near retirement and needed to continue in his position for just a little while longer.

Emma had Kathryn's illness to deal with. Isabel needed a lot of attention, too. Isabel witnessed the progression of her sister's illness. This affected her. She grew up quickly.

Mitch remembered one of the times when Angela was very ill. Emma sent him cookies and other items in the mail. He kind of appreciated them, but he was a teenager and thought he knew everything. He thought that he didn't need anyone. He didn't thank Emma. Mitch thought *guess I was rude.*

Emma's daughters did not like Mitch. They only remembered him from this period in their lives. They considered him to be a smart ass. Emma tried to talk to him several times on the phone and he brushed her off. Kathryn and Isabel saw their mother cry after one of those phone calls. They were angry with him and never forgot that night. Isabel told their mom, "someone should correct Mitchell."

Emma hugged them, "He doesn't understand. He just does not comprehend the circumstances. He is a male and a teenager, and he's hurting. I feel sorry for him. He stays at home alone when Luke is gone, and takes care of the house by himself."

Isabel always liked to speak to Luke on the phone. He was nice to her. He listened to her talk about the things going on in her life and what she was interested in or was studying. Isabel occasionally phoned Luke for advice as she was growing up. Luke usually said something she liked and she would follow his guidance.

Unknown to Emma and Luke, when left alone, Isabel phoned who she thought was her grandmother. Nothing offset the poisoning of her mind, and no antidote would ever be administered.

top hat

he waited for days outside my house

one day I thought he moved toward my home
instead he took a family from a dwelling up the road
where he selected another family some years ago

both multiple deaths were by car crashes
rumors began to circulate about the house

still   I wondered why the figure in the top hat lingered near my home
was his mission incomplete

the oblivious inhabitants of the area with their immortality coupons did
not wonder at his continued presence at their corner   but I did

I did not collect coupons
he only wanted one

later
my daughter died

--e. smith sleigh

cloak

The classroom was dark. In preparation for my presentation I reviewed the images on the screen. I was the only one there. I hit the remote and Mantegna's *Madonna and Child*, circa 1445, came up.

I choked back the tears as I looked at the magnificent painting about the love of a young mother for her child. This mother cradles her swaddled infant and gazes into the dark that surrounds them. She draws her baby closer.

In that moment, she sees his future. In a time to come she will lose her child, her infant, who resides on the altar of her arms. She pulls her cloak up and around the child in an attempt to protect them both from the shadows and the future that will separate them.

Kathryn was very ill at the time. I felt myself hold her as a baby. I, too, knew the fate of my child, her prognosis. I felt what Mantegna so aptly represented. I knew what the mother was feeling: it was an overwhelming, paralyzing sadness, a hard-metalic-tasting emptiness.

I turned off the projector. The classroom remained darkened while tears burned my cheeks.

"The day before Kathryn died she made me promise that I would pursue writing. I read some of my poetry to the children when they were younger.

She also asked me to continue to research her disease and find out as much as possible about her ancestors who carried the cystic fibrosis genes. Of course, I did what she asked. It helped me with mourning an unspeakable loss. I discovered so much about world history as a whole and her specific **heritage.**

Someday, perhaps, when I can think, concentrate, accept this reality, I may write again, but not now."

implosions

sometimes I'm…

this situation can only be defined by doubt heavy emotion
a shake through my body an urge for flight out a door
a window out of town state country

I always had options but now in the hard cold depressed
atmosphere of an imploded era a barren landscape bald
mountain no back up no option exists except exit

exist exit
exist
exit

I'm banging walls with my fists

d'oro thy don Dave

one day I will run into you I will not recognize you and you will
know it you jaded dated overrated over the rainbow
scarecrow follow the yellow brick road did you say you're not in
Kansas anymore old old post card from Leavenworth or was it OZ
and points north is it funny

talk to me now did you have all the fun no one expected you to have
you abused do you whisper it to yourself on those rare occasions
when you acknowledge the darkest shadow that moves across your
mirror officer and a what but you're a clean machine right

I told you "your daughter's dead"

from Egypt over the crackling phone, you said "that's too bad"

I remember, oh I remember:

July

I spent life in a
perfect day
doing nothing
enjoying the sounds of the earth

the golden sunshine
the sensuous heat
the laughter of my children

oh   summer linger here
and go with me
at my death

Mitch walked over to the sofa, sat down, and put his head on her shoulder. "This is hard, so hard. I am now living the consequences of **not knowing** my past."

After a while, he reached into his pocket and handed her an envelope. "This is addressed to you, uhh, Isabel from Luke and Emma. It fills in the blanks. The letter explains why we weren't told about our true identities and why we were allowed to believe a different family history."

Isabel opened the letter but didn't remove it from the envelope. She recognized her mother's handwriting. She held the letter for several minutes. Isabel went into the large center hall closet and pulled out a small flashlight and looked inside. She found two folded sheets of paper along with a photo. At length she summoned the courage to look down. She began to read.

Dear One,

Do you remember how you were drawn to Luke when you were a child? It was only natural because he is your father. I am sorry Luke and I did not tell you earlier.

Just before Dave and I were scheduled to return to the States, Luke and I met in Copenhagen. He read a paper at a university symposium.

We were together in Denmark for several days. Copenhagen was beautiful and we made you there, dear Isabel. Luke and I were delighted when we found out I was pregnant. We wanted to marry, but it wasn't possible for a long time. I wanted you so much. I went through a lot to convince Dave you were his. Kathryn *is* his child.

The night you were born, Luke was with us. Dave was on temporary duty, hundreds of miles away. I didn't really know anyone within our new military community.

I had no one to help other than Luke, who flew in to be with us.

We told people he was my father. So, it was easy enough. Your birth pleased him so much. When he saw you, he cried for the third time in his life. You were a beautiful baby and we were so very proud of you. Luke followed every minute of your childhood.

Luke and I decided we would tell you that we are your parents when you became an adult. I couldn't wait to say you were ours, but then you left us. Afterwards, the timing never seemed right.

As you know, Dave and I were married quite a while without having children. I knew I could have them because I had Mitchell when I was in college. He is my child, too, Isabel. He is mine, and Luke's.

There's not an easy way to say this. Mitch is your brother. I fell in love with Luke when he was my teacher. I was a young student. I hope by now you are aware of the circumstances. I had Mitch when I dropped out of college for a year. During that time, Luke and I discovered how difficult it would be to explain what happened between us, a young student and a professor.

At the time of Mitch's birth and under the strict university employment standards, Luke would have lost his job and his career. We would both lose so much. Because of the mores of the time, Mitch's career could not be assured.

We decided that Luke would ask Angela, who couldn't have children, if she would raise Mitch. She thought Mitch's parents were students on campus. Luke extracted a signed agreement from her that she would be his mother. There was no adoption.

Angela agreed not to tell Mitch or anyone else about his true origins. She agreed but countered with some stiff terms of her own including no divorce from Luke, no other women, it went on and on. She backed him into a corner.

I know you aren't fond of Mitch but he *is* your brother. Luke and I were delighted we had a boy and a girl. We hope you like having a sister *and* a brother.

We vowed one day we would have our children under the same roof. We wanted to give our children a whole family and their history. It almost happened. I was so disappointed when it did not.

I hope at some point you will forgive Mitch. Luke and I also ask your forgiveness. We apologize for not giving you the truth earlier.

We wrote Mitch a similar letter.

If you are reading this letter, then you are under unusual circumstances. Please be careful. I ask you to protect yourself and those you love. Know this, we love you. Our thoughts are with you.

All our Love,

Emma and Luke

Oh, one more thing, Isabel, if a man name Linus contacts you, then something happened and you're in trouble. Listen to him. He will help you no matter where you are or what you need."

Isabel looked down at the photo of Emma and Luke in the Tivoli Gardens, Copenhagen. Tears welled in her eyes.

"These are my parents, my true parents."

a high price for moonlight

night rises in me like a shadow beast
night rises cascades down me
                                        like a black silk gown
night rises within the course of my sorrows
night pours through me
                                        like multiple psyches

I dwell in the monochrome void
               the eddying gulf stream
                                        the yawning chasm
night buries itself in me
                                        like a gemmed
                                        silvery ceremonial knife
               like loss
                        lost love
                        lost children
                                        a malevolent mother
night rises and the damned in their dark torment do not want to be me

night rises and calls forth this lament
                                        this yowl down the staircase
up the brackish river
                                        along the unpaved path

waves of my wail and grief flow out of me
                                        they form circular patterns
                                        in the air above me
my existence suffers the nights
                                        I'm seeking a light
                                        I'm seeking a last night away
                                        from the shadow beasts

Part V
Later Life

lacking a natural, usual, or appropriate covering

bare headed
bare arm
bare fisted
bare chested
bare breasted
bare assed
bare naked
bare bones
  laid bare
bare apartment
bare room
bare walls
bare necessities
bare facts
bare landscape
bare trees
bare hands
   riding bareback
bared secrets
bare of all safeguards

nude   bald
stripped
barren
barred
baring fangs

a bald mountain
a bare two hours away

chanson luxe

winter arrives   someone dies
emotions concealed and avalanching
images carefully curated
still feels like there's something missing
was hers a comprehensible world
it was once a life
that could brighten the skies

where I dwell   the daylight hours
are grey then sunny then grey again
these days I crave the sunny morns

dangerous to think about what's happening
what is changing   pivotal forces impact life
feels like more than just a series of events
small forces crash life
large forces crush

somewhere there's a sun
of not deeper circumstance

la chanson luxe

fractured her hip

I fell   I held a four month old newspaper printout in my
shaking hand   no one told me

I knew she was the cause of my fall   her   the harsh one
the screamer   pelting me with fists clenched   murmuring
ridicule   sometimes   when I wasn't there   guilt and
criticism delivered at supersonic speeds   abuser   full of deceit
undermining my life   attempting to take my child

why wouldn't I fall with no floor underneath me
I carried her epitaph in my hand   her life of hate shortened
to 200 words   all those words she spewed   now her life is
condensed into so short an essay

excited and sad to finally obtain freedom   from the demon
the worst antagonist in my life   her family and husband always
offered an excuse for her   they withheld their disdain   no one
spoke the unspeakable

the injury isn't my hip   but it was her broken hip that killed her
now I punish myself with this fall but for what   what did I
do this time   I lived   that's all it took   I live

good bye you abusing   ass

at dawn   I was sore   but I walked
I watched the sun rise
and drew my first deep breath

repeat after me

"we keep things to ourselves
no one needs to know about this
everything is fine   we're fine   remember that"

I've decided not to keep these things to myself

she left me nothing and gave my estranged
older daughter everything

that was my mother's legacy to me
the nurturing of loathing in Isabel
that keeps my surviving child and I
apart

coats   Montreal

singing on the frozen sidewalk tundra
to a syncopated humming of lights
turned icy blue   in winter

breathing in
a wintry wind that locks up my lungs
on a chilled to the bone Wednesday
in the auto free zone

thinking about drinking frigid vodka
searching for some answers
seeking solutions in the bottom
of something icy
cold

I never liked their explanations
perhaps   *it is* just procreation
is a *is*
I believe it's something else

send in the chill
the troops
the black and white photos
the stolen time loops
the stolen cases of swill

the juggernauts
with nasty knots of not-good will

thoughts in early morning

dawn approaches
with the roar
of a cicada chorus

will this day
of my existence
be offered to me

or

do I have to take it

“The files!” He paused to catch his breath. “We stored the papers here, in the lodge. I don’t know if they will understand what we discovered, especially the Americans.”

“Be careful. Mitchell, you must find someone, someone you can trust, to, I, I'm sorry, I can't help you with, when you're not working on the papers, always put them away, in the safe, or, be, care, full…” He couldn't finish. He lost his breath.

Luke Seebeck lay back on his pillow exhausted. *I want to sleep, I want to wrap my body around her and sleep.* Fatigue coursed through his body. He was weary in his mind, and heart. After a couple of minutes, he coaxed his body up on an elbow to look straight at his son.

He whispered, "Son, I love you. Thank you for, try to find Emma, try to find her daughter, I have to tell you something, ahhh, please try to understand our circumstances. Remember what we think we seek frequently bears little resemblance to what we will eventually find." His remaining strength left him and he slumped down into the covers.

"I will, Dad, I, we, love you, too." Mitch looked away for a moment. "Don't talk now."

Mitchell couldn't think of anything else to say. He took a couple of steps toward the window. He looked outside at the lake just to rest his mind, but the water was restless and rough. Mitch thought *white caps, not a good sign.*

What do I do now?

"Emma?" He heard his father's raspy voice. After a few moments, his father called out for her again, "Emma...?"

Luke coughed.

Mitch listened to Luke for a second. He heard his father expel all the air in his lungs. He recognized the sound. It announced the end of a life. He frequently heard the rattle when he was younger and a medic.

He rushed over to Luke's bed.
"N, nooo. No!"

Mitchell took his father's hand and checked his wrist and neck for a pulse. *No pulse.* He leaned toward Luke's nose and mouth and listened. *Nothing. Dad's chest isn't moving.*

He shook his head. *I didn't realize Dad was so sick. Poor Dad, he waited for me, he waited until I could sit down beside his bed and listen to what he had to say.*

Mitch felt relief for his father, and for himself. He thought, *is this selfish? I don't know. I'm glad he died at home.*

I have nothing but questions. What disease caused him so much pain? Why didn't I know about this? Why wasn't I told about the papers? How dangerous, or for that matter how significant, could some historical research be? Where is Emma? If she's alive, she should be here right now.

Mitch lowered his head and stared at the floor. After a few seconds, his eyes rested on Luke's body.

"What the hell, my father, oh, Dad, what just happened here?"

He lowered himself into the overstuffed chair by his father's bedside. His tears fell onto the rug. He put his head in his hands and his elbows on his thighs and rocked back and forth.

Soon Mitchell noticed how quiet the house was. He looked up and scanned the dim rooms beyond the kitchen. *This is crazy. At any moment, I expect to see Luke and Emma stride through the kitchen door.*

Something, some need to be near the things his dad touched compelled Mitch into the office where his father spent a great deal of his time. He entered the room and paused at the desk.

Family and travel photos were arranged on the desktop and in the bookshelves. They were scattered among the certificates and degrees. Photos also hung on the wall behind the desk chair.

He looked around the large desktop. His dad positioned a stack of color-coded index files beside his notebook. 'Go through these files first.' The files contained, among other things, typed pages from Emma's journals, memoirs, short stories, research and poetry.

On a sheet of paper at the top of one of the files, Luke wrote:

"Just keep in mind this is a fictionalized memoir in so many ways. It presents Emma's life as rather easy, when in fact it never was."

Emma:

"I am older now.

I was unable to fulfill a good number
of my dreams.

I'm alright and not.

I still adore you, Luke, my love.

I miss our children."

transports

in a cityscape a wailing
train whistle echoes
off the buildings and concrete
it resembles a barge horn
that bounces off riverbanks
islands   the watercourse inlets

during the dark of night
through the stillness
comes the lonely moan
of each   the train   the barge

the sounds evoke a need to escape
to flee the agony of misspent time
wrong love   lost loves
regrets turned into sounds
that bound   from ears to head
to heart and back again
mournful howls invade the body
drench cheeks and prick at veins

it is a walk   a run   into
the piercing nothingness
into the sounds' solitary emptiness
the yowls diminish while the transports
move away to the distant distance
vanished instants

within the *adieu*   their squalls are
forestalled   somehow
but wailing   waiting
don't expect an ending

Made in the USA
Monee, IL
01 September 2020

40792913R00067